HAL•LEONARD

GUITAR
PLAY•ALONG

Pop METAL

VOL. 55

T0078967

Tracking, mixing, and mastering by
Jake Johnson & Bill Maynard at Paradyme Productions
All guitars by Doug Boduch
Bass by Tom McGirr
Keyboards by Warren Wiegratz
Drums by Scott Schroedl

ISBN: 978-1-4234-0065-3

Visit Hal Leonard Online at **www.halleonard.com**

HAL•LEONARD®
CORPORATION
7777 W. BLUEMOUND RD. P.O. BOX 13819
MILWAUKEE, WISCONSIN 53213

Guitar Notation Legend

THE MUSICAL STAFF shows pitches and rhythms and is divided by bar lines into measures. Pitches are named after the first seven letters of the alphabet.

TABLATURE graphically represents the guitar fingerboard. Each horizontal line represents a string, and each number represents a fret.

4th string, 2nd fret   1st & 2nd strings open, played together   open D chord

HALF-STEP BEND: Strike the note and bend up 1/2 step.

WHOLE-STEP BEND: Strike the note and bend up one step.

GRACE NOTE BEND: Strike the note and bend up as indicated. The first note does not take up any time.

SLIGHT (MICROTONE) BEND: Strike the note and bend up 1/4 step.

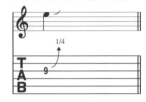

BEND AND RELEASE: Strike the note and bend up as indicated, then release back to the original note. Only the first note is struck.

PRE-BEND: Bend the note as indicated, then strike it.

VIBRATO: The string is vibrated by rapidly bending and releasing the note with the fretting hand.

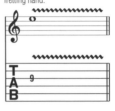

PALM MUTING: The note is partially muted by the pick hand lightly touching the string(s) just before the bridge.

HAMMER-ON: Strike the first (lower) note with one finger, then sound the higher note (on the same string) with another finger by fretting it without picking.

PULL-OFF: Place both fingers on the notes to be sounded. Strike the first note and without picking, pull the finger off to sound the second (lower) note.

LEGATO SLIDE: Strike the first note and then slide the same fret-hand finger up or down to the second note. The second note is not struck.

SHIFT SLIDE: Same as legato slide, except the second note is struck.

PINCH HARMONIC: The note is fretted normally and a harmonic is produced by adding the edge of the thumb or the tip of the index finger of the pick hand to the normal pick attack.

TRILL: Very rapidly alternate between the notes indicated by continuously hammering on and pulling off.

TAPPING: Hammer ("tap") the fret indicated with the pick-hand index or middle finger and pull off to the note fretted by the fret hand.

NATURAL HARMONIC: Strike the note while the fret-hand lightly touches the string directly over the fret indicated.

TREMOLO PICKING: The note is picked as rapidly and continuously as possible.

VIBRATO BAR DIVE AND RETURN: The pitch of the note or chord is dropped a specified number of steps (in rhythm) then returned to the original pitch.

VIBRATO BAR SCOOP: Depress the bar just before striking the note, then quickly release the bar.

VIBRATO BAR DIP: Strike the note and then immediately drop a specified number of steps, then release back to the original pitch.

Additional Musical Definitions

 (accent) • Accentuate note (play it louder)

 (staccato) • Play the note short

D.S. al Coda • Go back to the sign (𝄋), then play until the measure marked *"To Coda"*, then skip to the section labelled *"Coda."*

D.C. al Fine • Go back to the beginning of the song and play until the measure marked *"Fine"* (end).

Fill • Label used to identify a brief melodic figure which is to be inserted into the arrangement.

N.C. • Instrument is silent (drops out).

 • Repeat measures between signs.

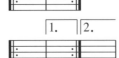 • When a repeated section has different endings, play the first ending only the first time and the second ending only the second time.

VOL. 55

CONTENTS

Beautiful Girls

Words and Music by David Lee Roth, Edward Van Halen, Alex Van Halen and Michael Anthony

Tune down 1/2 step:
(low to high) E♭-A♭-D♭-G♭-B♭-E♭

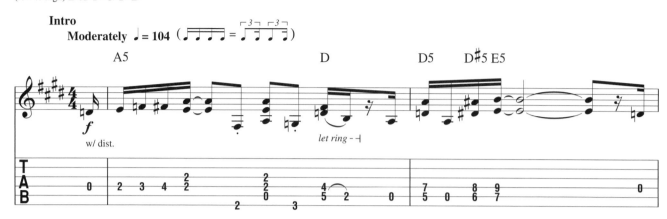

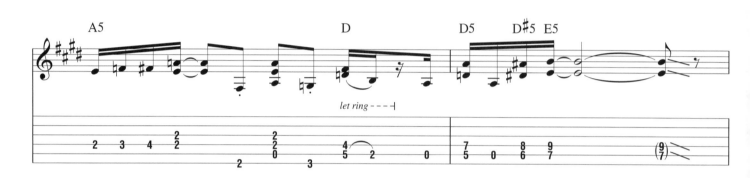

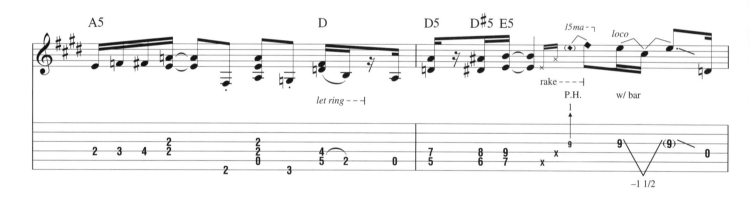

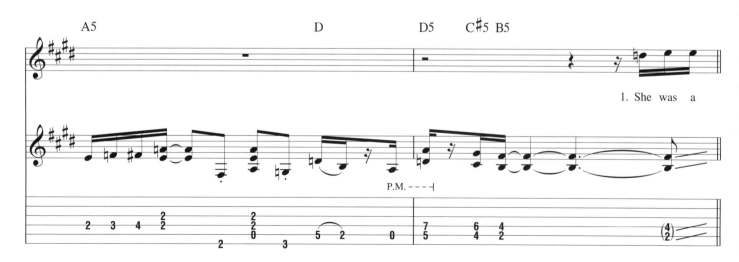

1. She was a

*Played as even sixteenth notes.

7

Interlude

Spoken: Sit down right —— here.

Sung: Oo, —— la, —— la! —

let ring

w/ bar

let ring

let ring

I think I got it now.

Harm.

let ring P.M.

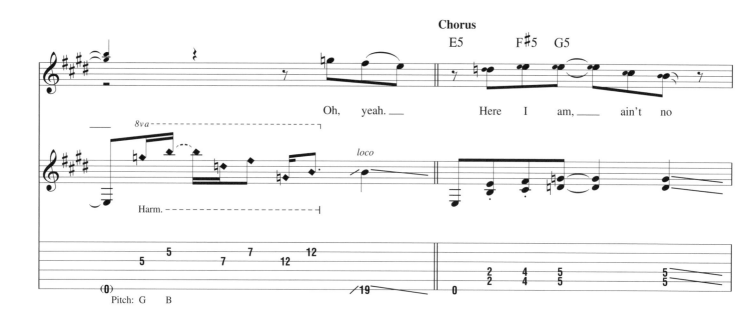

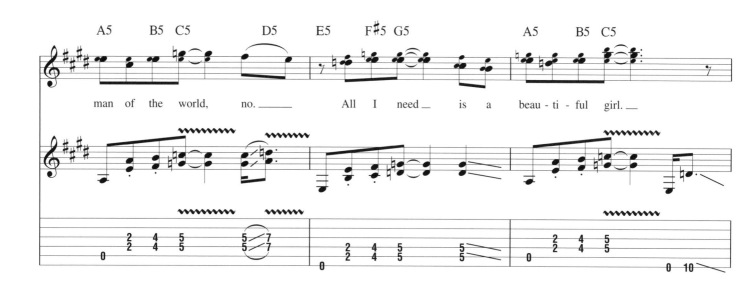

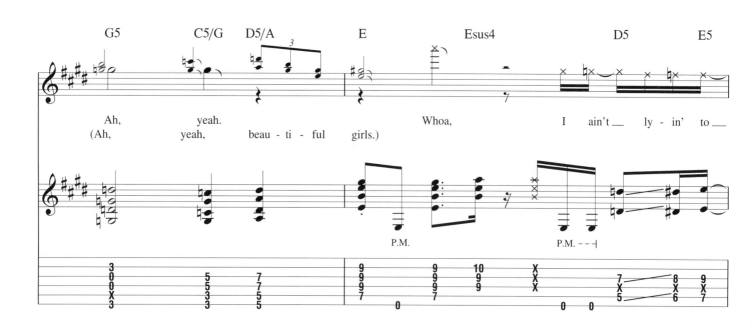

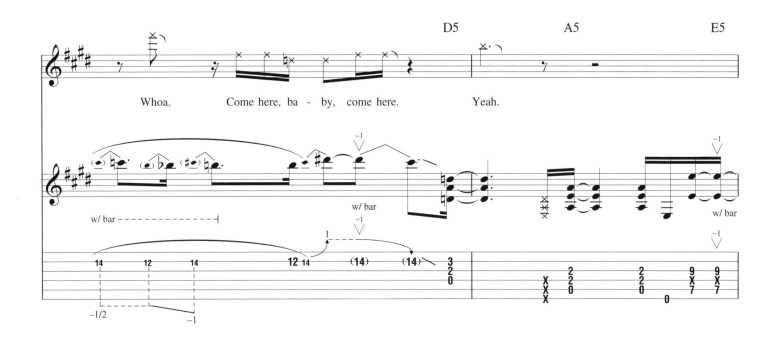

Whoa. Come here, ba - by, come here. Yeah.

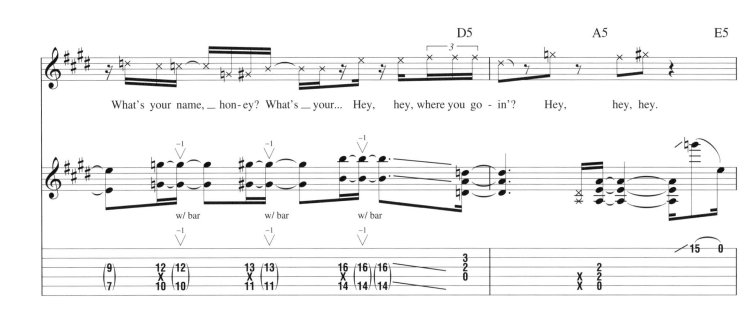

What's your name, __ hon-ey? What's __ your... Hey, hey, where you go - in'? Hey, hey, hey.

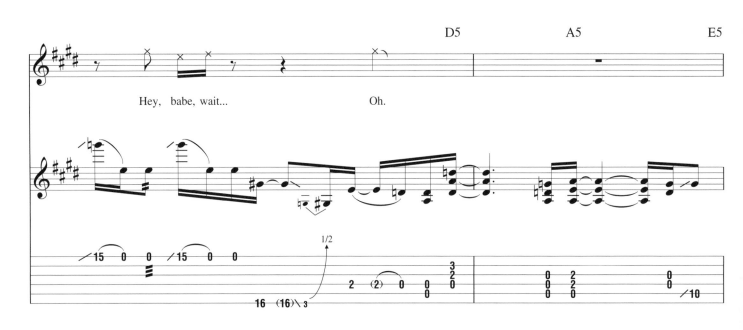

Hey, babe, wait... Oh.

*Kissing sound

15

Cherry Pie

Words and Music by Jani Lane

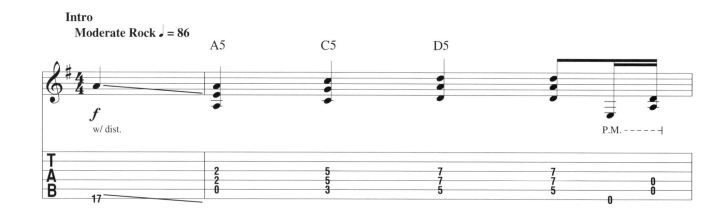

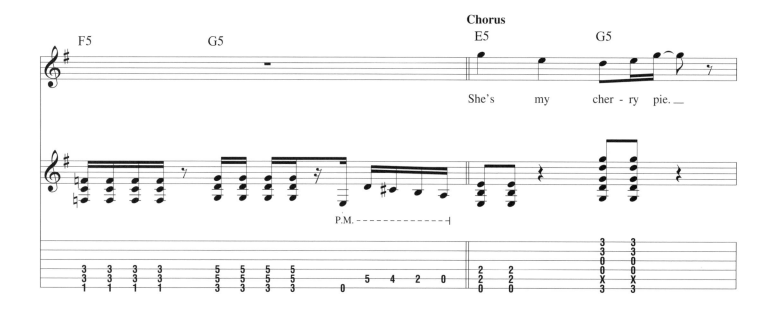

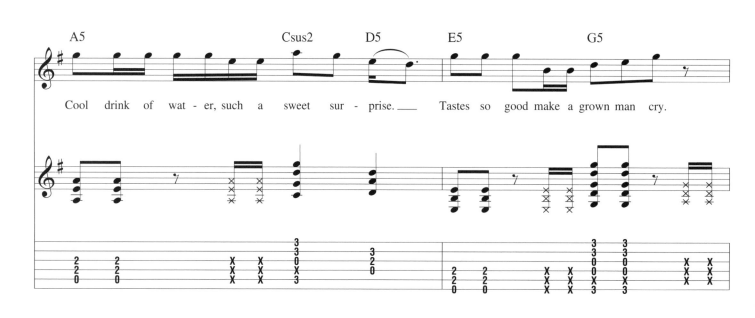

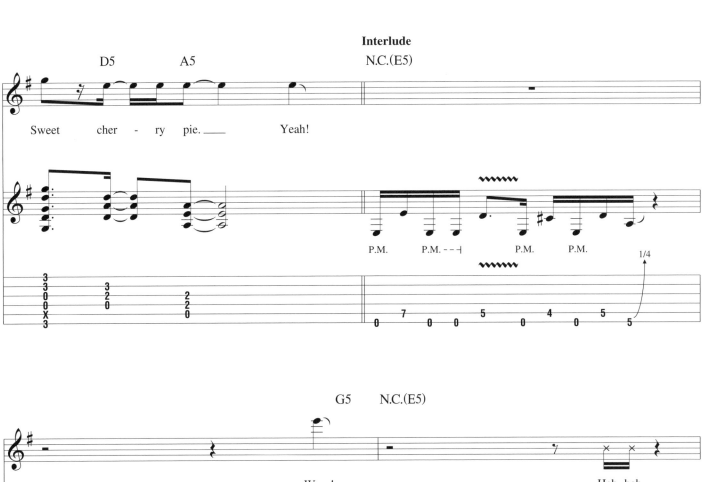

Interlude

D5   A5   N.C.(E5)

Sweet cher - ry pie. ___ Yeah!

G5   N.C.(E5)

Wow!   Heh, heh.

Verse

G5   A5   E5

1. Well, swing-in' on the front porch, swing-in' on the lawn.

Guitar Solo

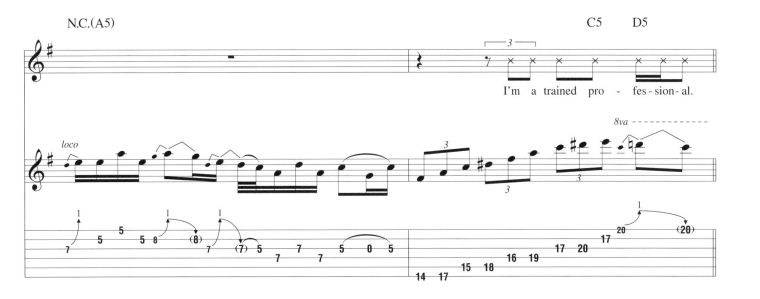

N.C.(A5)　　　　　　　　　　　　　　　　　　　　　　　　　　C5　　D5

I'm a trained pro - fes - sion - al.

Verse

4. Swing-in' in the bath-room, swing-in' on the floor. Swing-in' so hard, _ for-got to lock the door. _

In　walk her dad-dy stand-in' six　foot　four, said,"You ain't gon-na swing with my daugh-ter no more."

23

Outro-Chorus

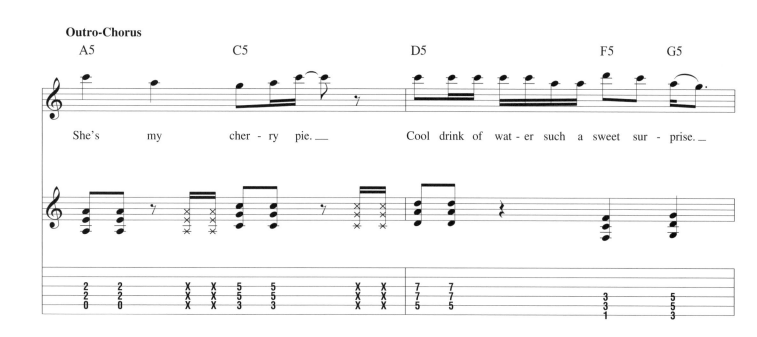

She's my cher - ry pie. ___ Cool drink of wat - er such a sweet sur - prise. ___

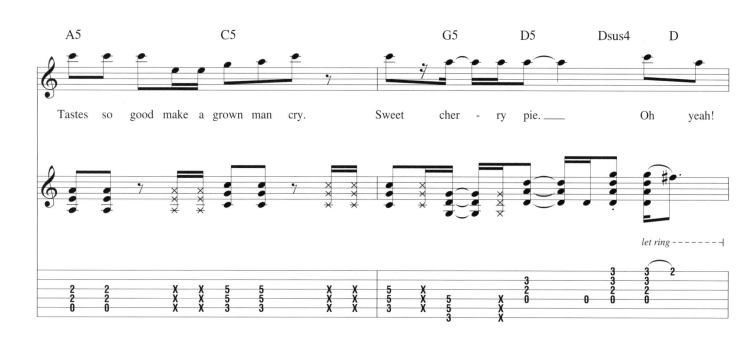

Tastes so good make a grown man cry. Sweet cher - ry pie. ___ Oh yeah!

let ring - - - - - - - -

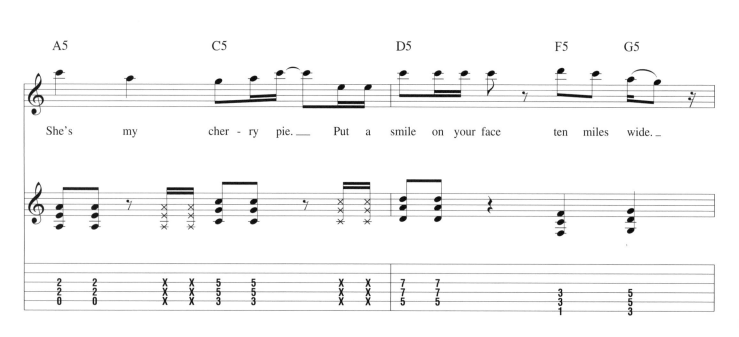

She's my cher - ry pie. ___ Put a smile on your face ten miles wide. _

Get the Funk Out

Words and Music by Nuno Bettencourt and Gary Cherone

Tune down 1/2 step:
(low to high) E♭-A♭-D♭-G♭-B♭-E♭

Intro
Moderate Rock ♩ = 108

(Drums & Bass)

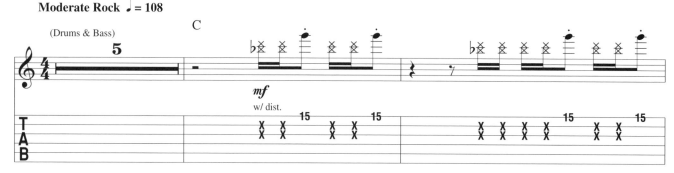

w/ dist.

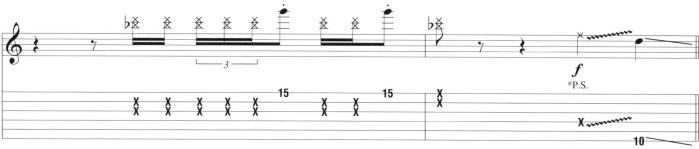

*P.S.

*Rub edge of pick up the string,
producing a scratchy sound.

Verse

1. If you don't like what you see here, _____ no - bod - y wants to take you
2. *See additional lyrics*

P.M. P.M. P.M.

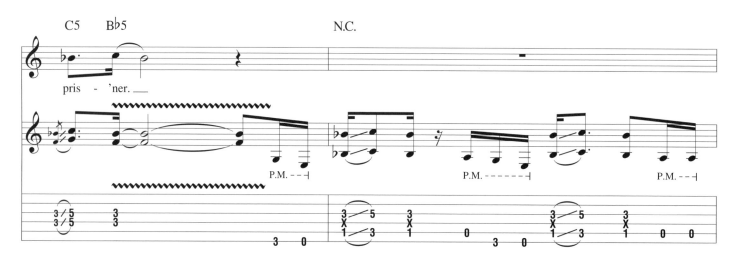

pris - 'ner. _____

N.C.

P.M. P.M. P.M.

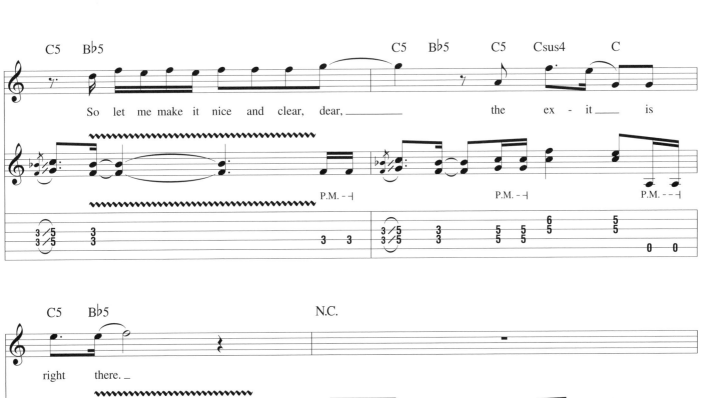

So let me make it nice and clear, dear, _____ the ex-it ___ is

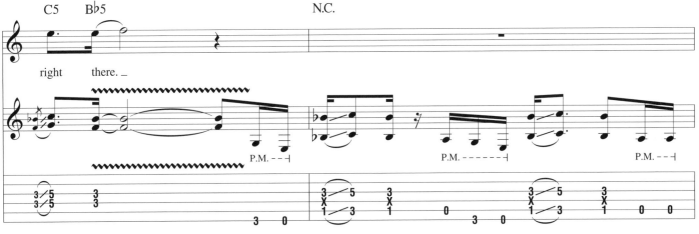

right there. _

I don't _ mean to be rude, dude, _____ but you bet-ter change your

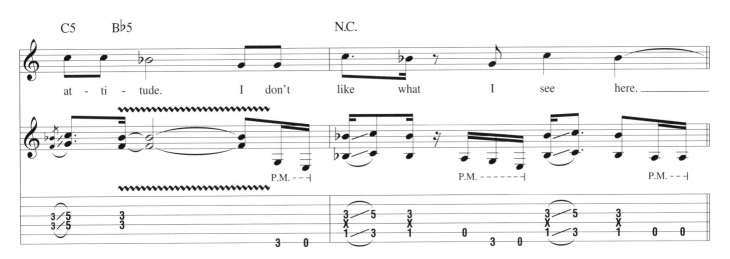

at-ti-tude. I don't like what I see here. _____

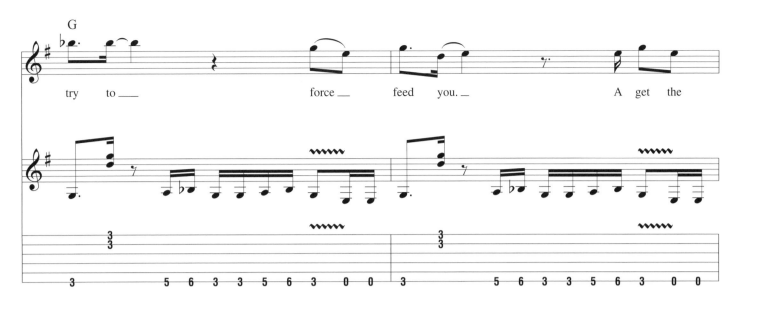

try to __ force _ feed you. _ A get the

1.

funk out. _ Hey, Pat - rick!

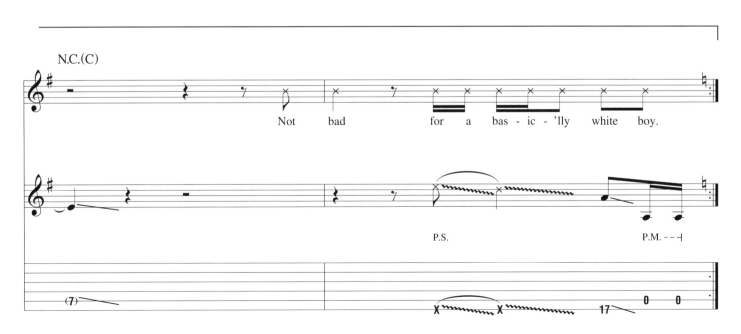

Not bad for a bas - ic - 'lly white boy.

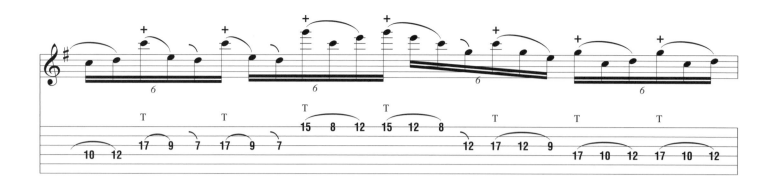

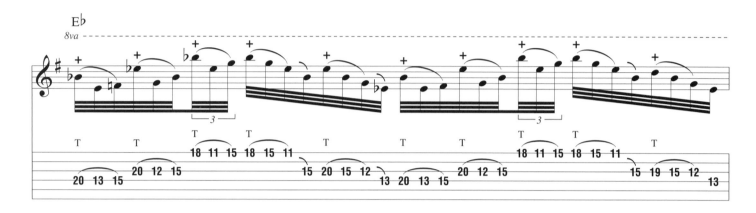

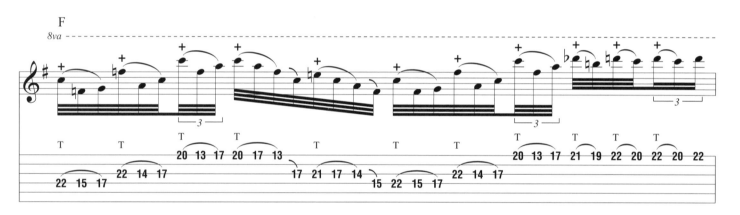

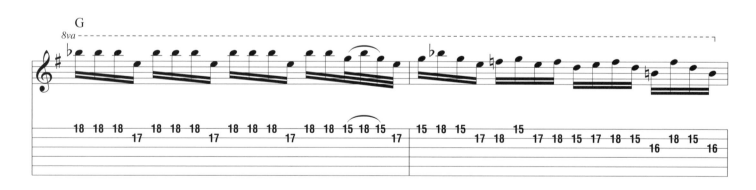

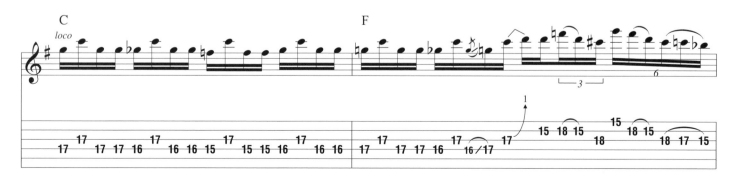

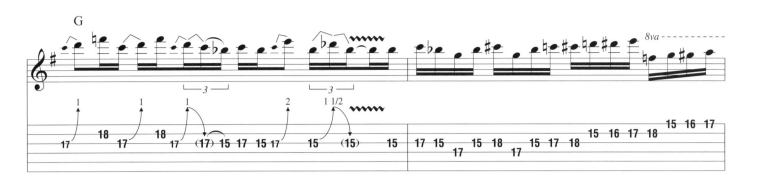

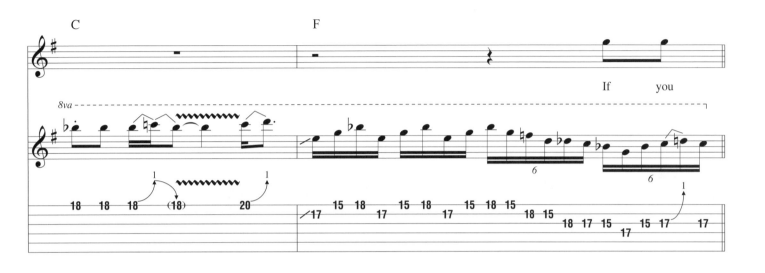

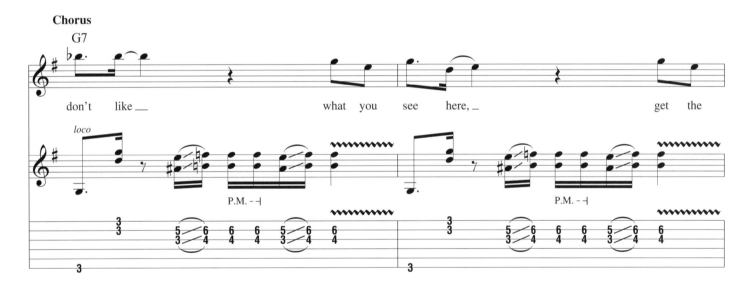

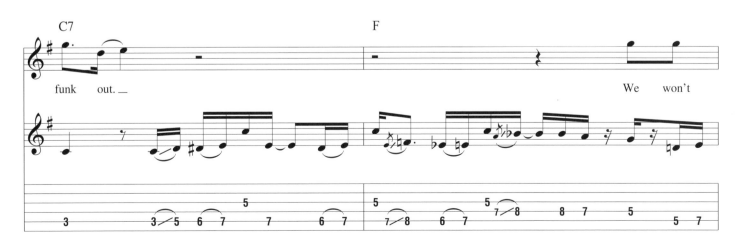

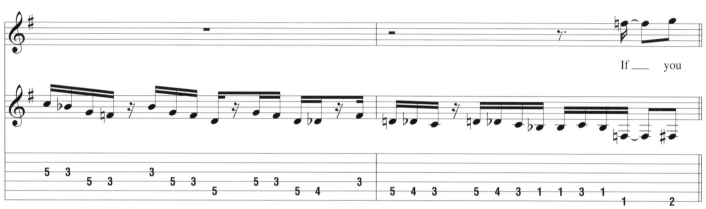

Outro-Chorus

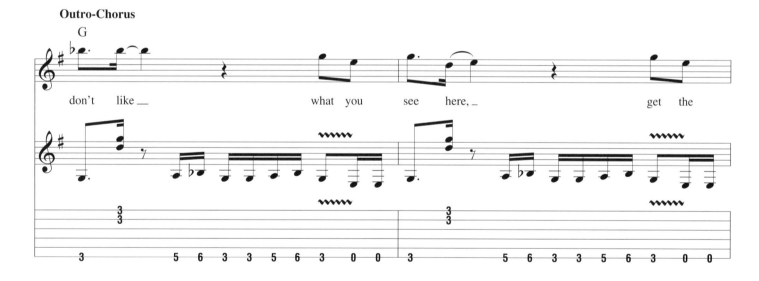

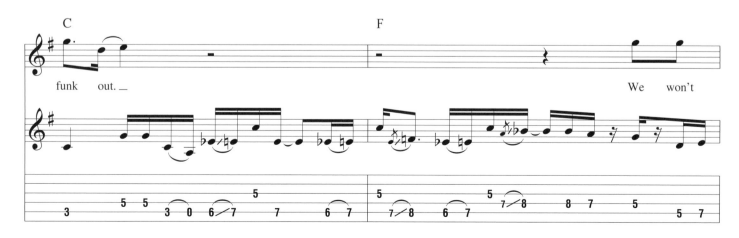

Additional Lyrics

2. You can't please ev'rybody,
   But ev'rybody cannot please me.
   I don't like what I see here.
   That's why I do what I want to.
   So why don't you do,
   Do it to, a do it to me, hey.
   And if you don't like what you see,
   You can always leave the country.
   Yeah, yeah, yeah, yeah, oh.

Here I Go Again

Words and Music by Bernie Marsden and David Coverdale

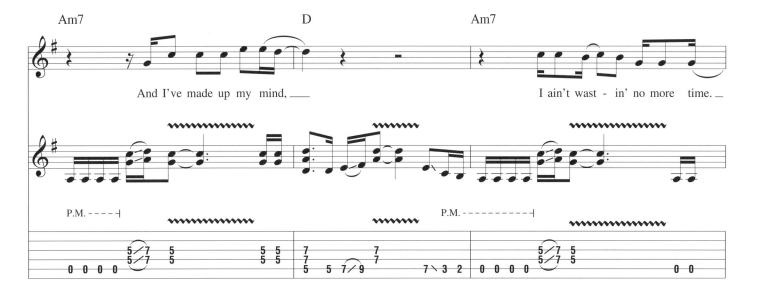

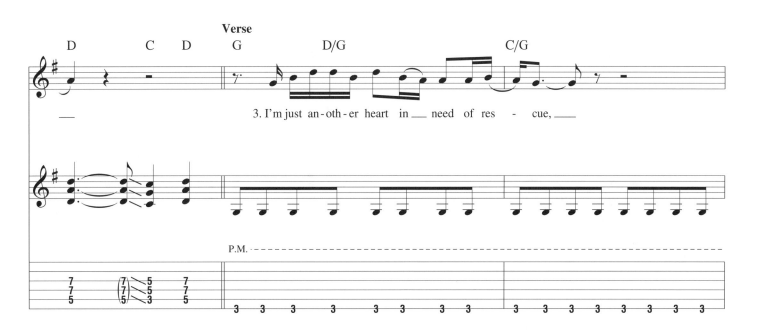

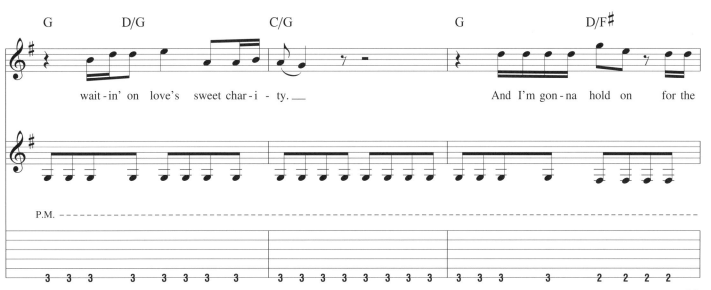

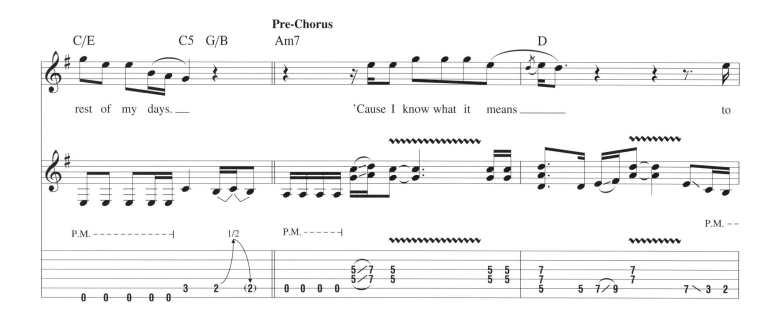

Pre-Chorus

rest of my days. ___ 'Cause I know what it means ___ to

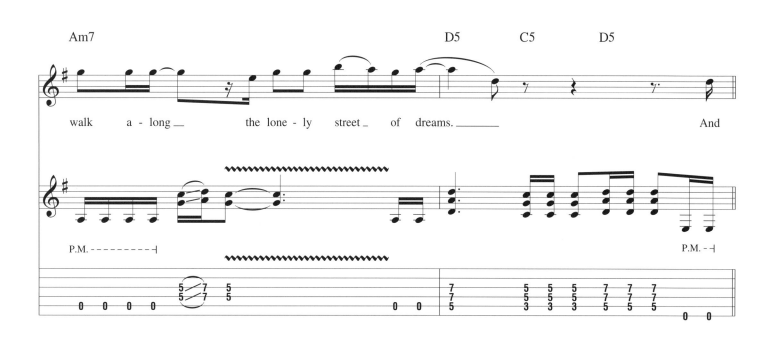

walk a - long ___ the lone - ly street ___ of dreams. ___ And

Chorus

here I go a - gain ___ on my own, ___ go - in' down the on - ly road ___ I've ev - er known. ___

Like a drift-er I ___ was born ___ to walk a-lone. ___

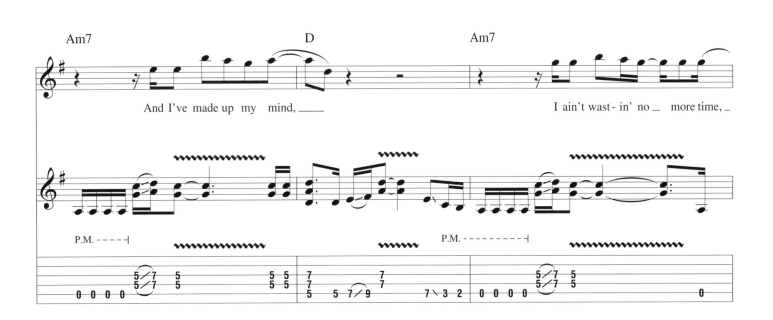

And I've made up my mind, ___

I ain't wast-in' no ___ more time, ___

Bridge

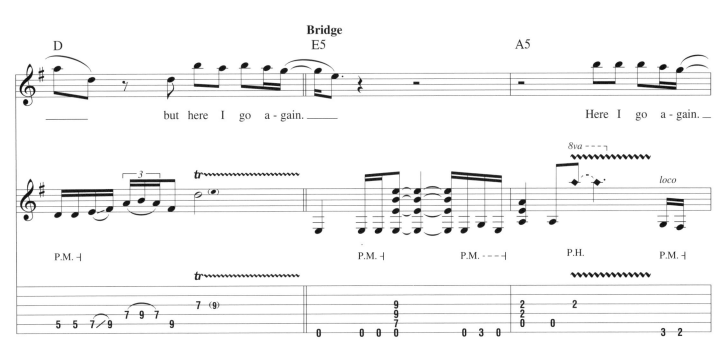

but here I go a-gain. ___

Here I go a-gain. ___

Here I go a-gain.

Here I go.

Guitar Solo

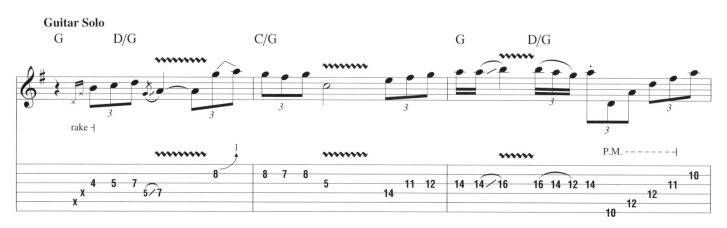

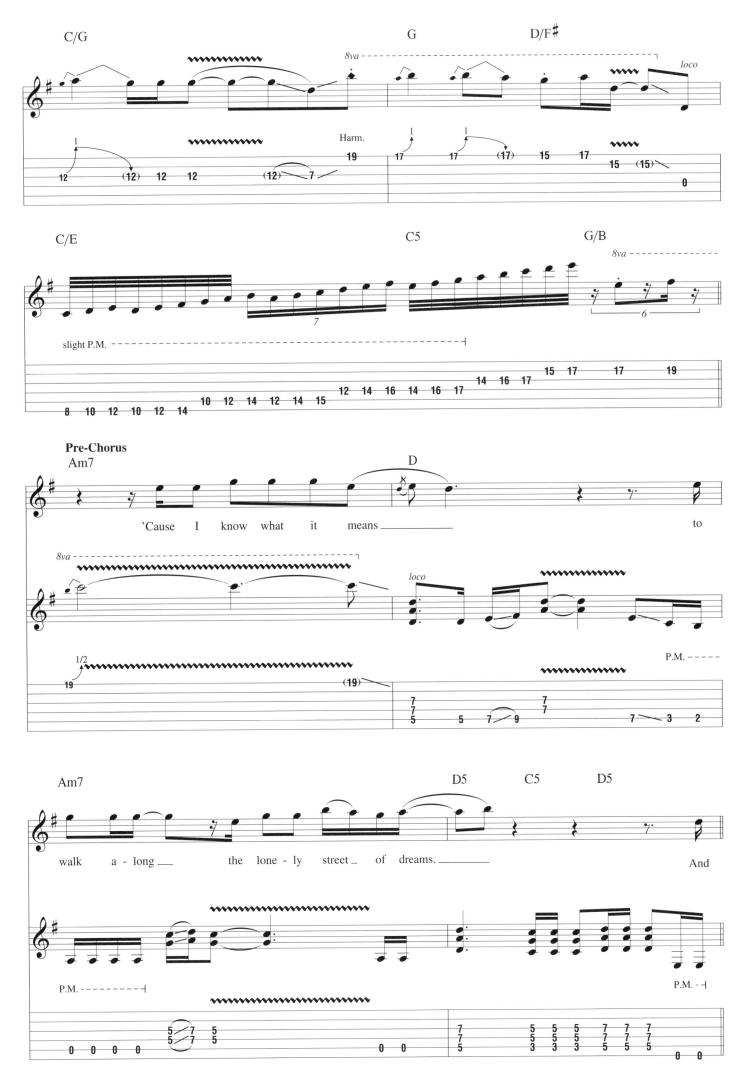

Chorus

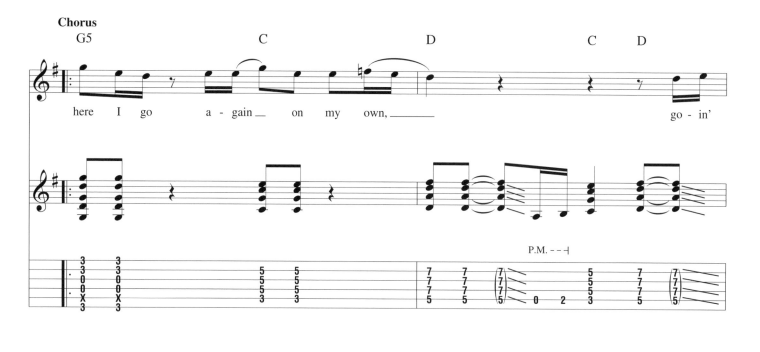

here I go a-gain___ on my own,___ go-in'

down the on — ly road___ I've ev-er known.___ Like a drift-er I___ was born___ to walk a-lone.___

{ And I've made up my mind,___
{ 'Cause I know what it means___ to

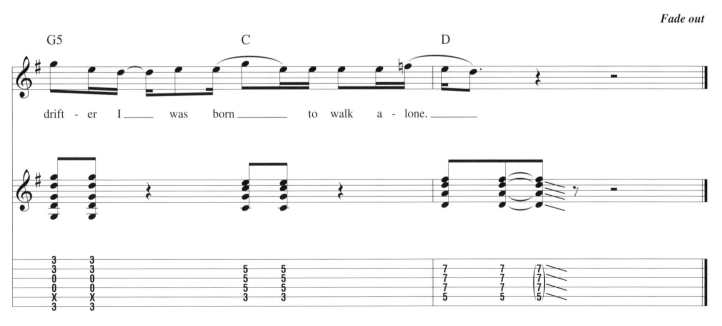

Photograph

Words and Music by Joe Elliott, Steve Clark, Peter Willis, Richard Savage, Richard Allen and Robert Lange

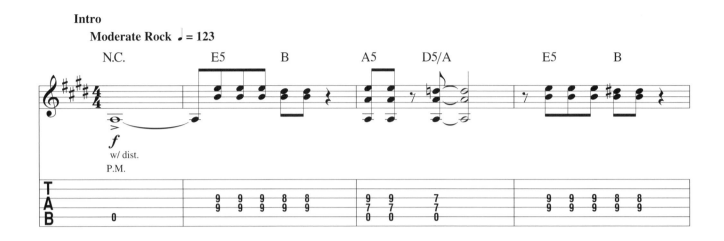

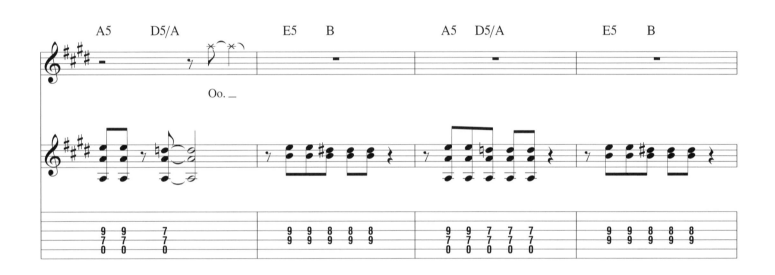

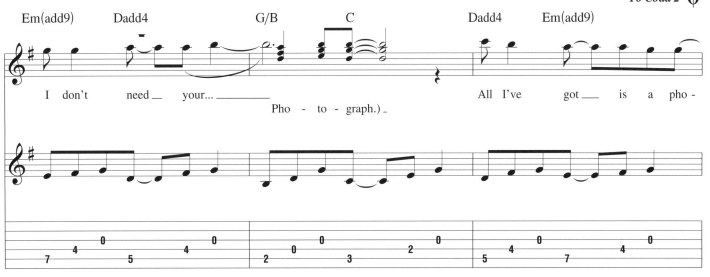

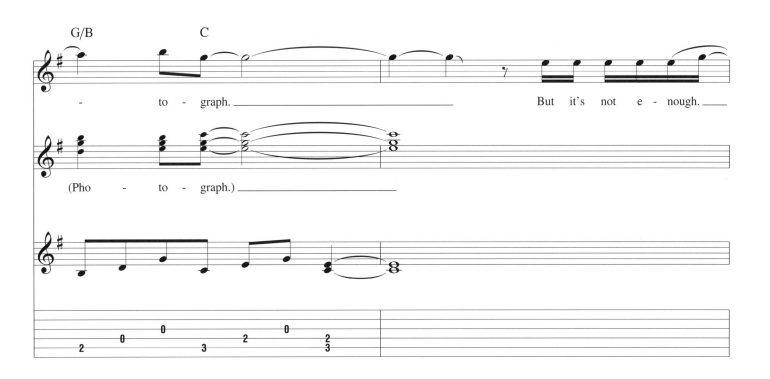

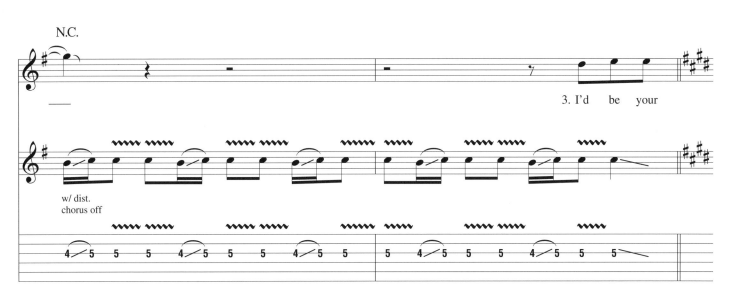

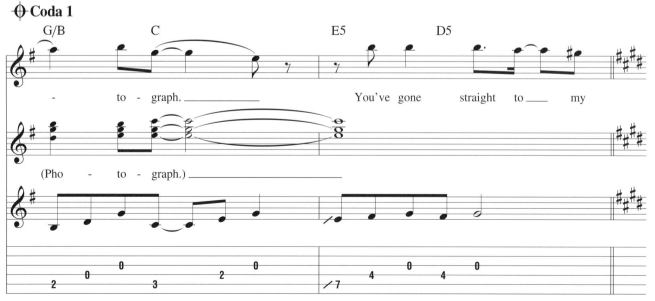

Interlude

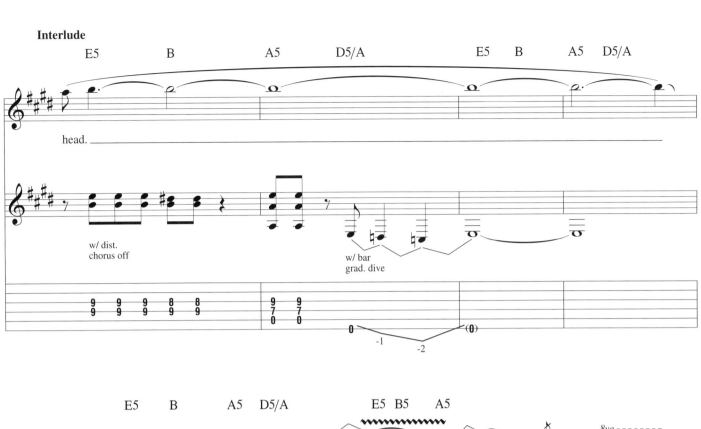

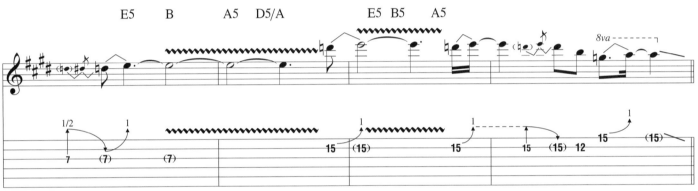

Guitar Solo

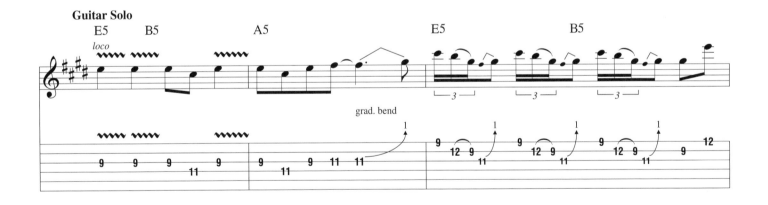

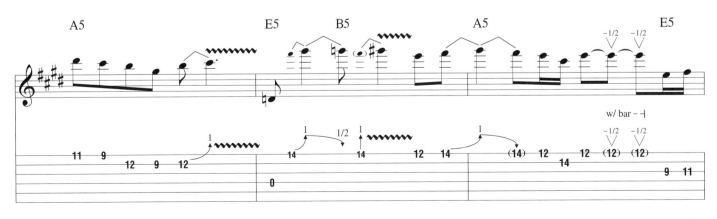

⊕ Coda 2

Gradually lift P.M.

Outro

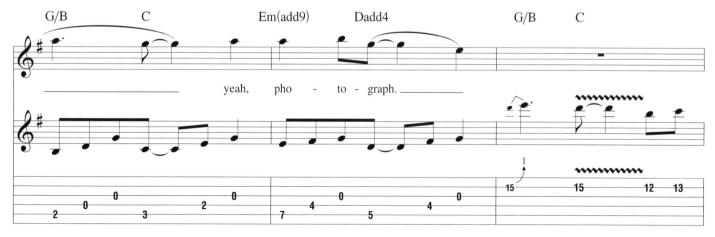

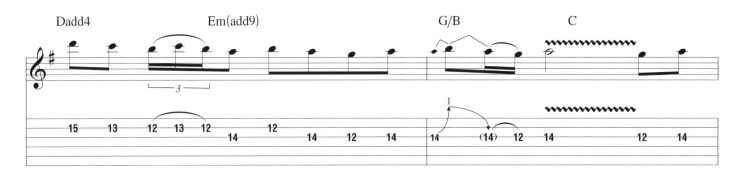

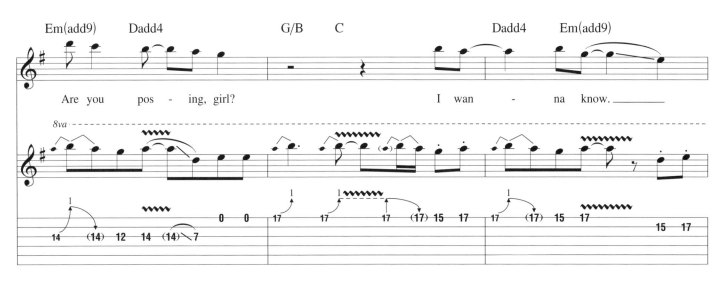

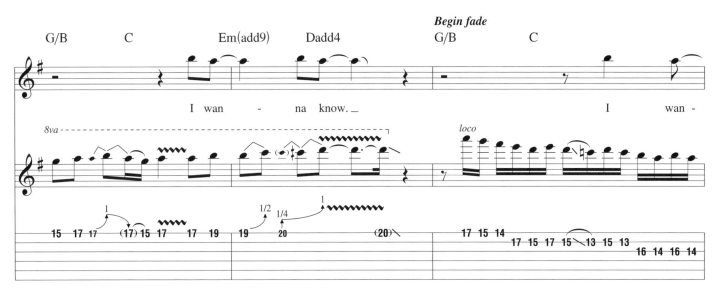

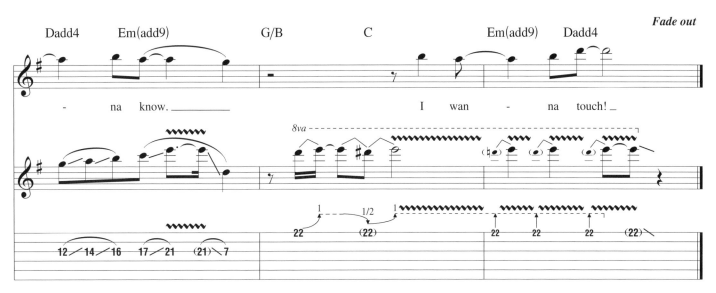

Turn Up the Radio

Words and Music by Steve Isham, Steve Lynch, Steven Plunkett, Randy Rand and Keni Richards

Tune down 1/2 step:
(low to high) E♭-A♭-D♭-G♭-B♭-E♭

Intro
Moderate Rock ♩ = 113

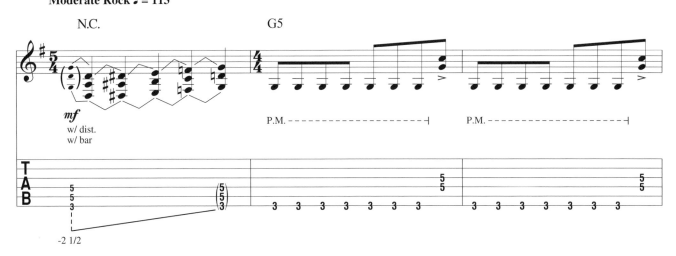

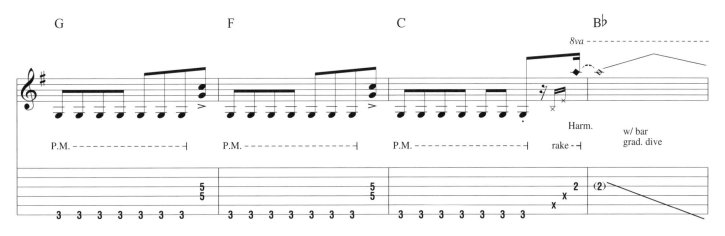

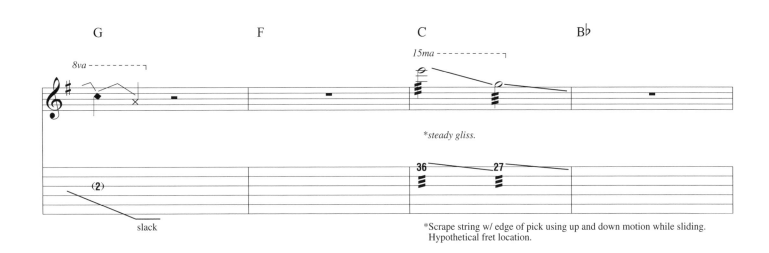

*Scrape string w/ edge of pick using up and down motion while sliding.
Hypothetical fret location.

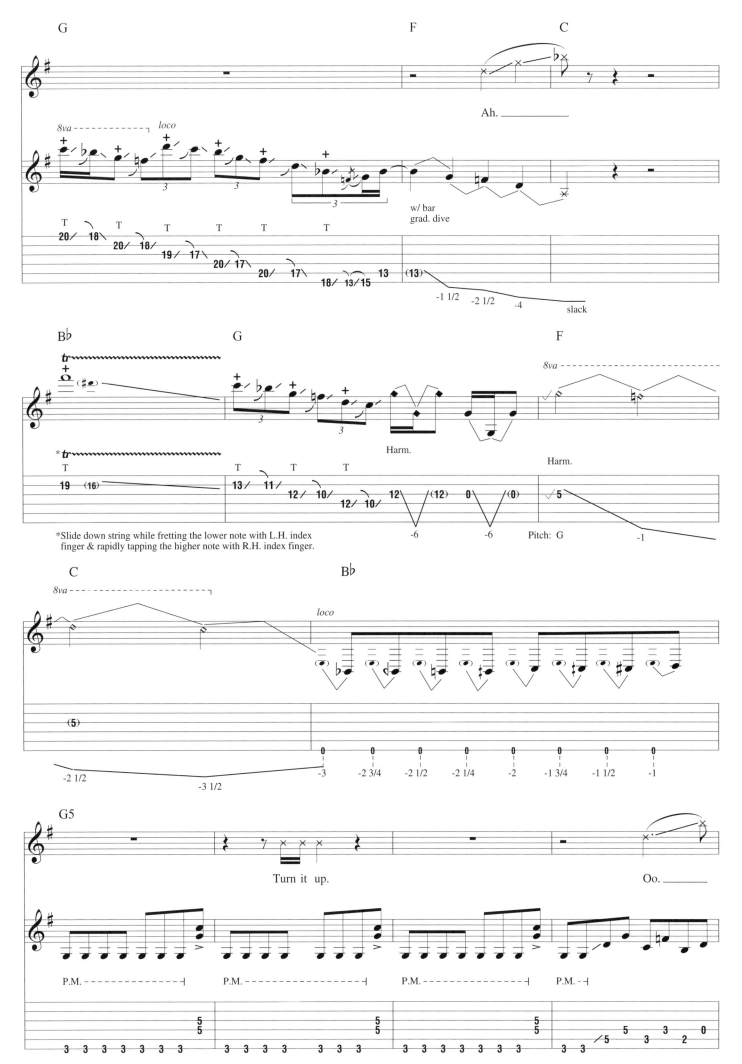

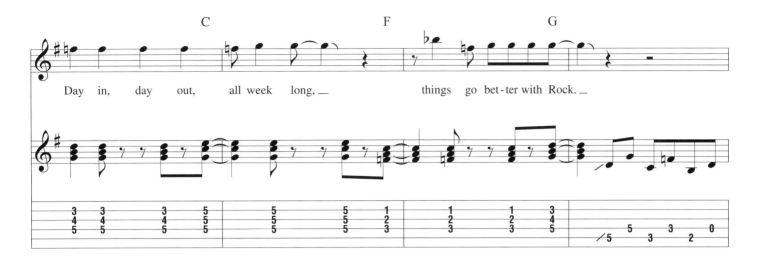

Day in, day out, all week long, __ things go bet-ter with Rock. __

The on - ly time I turn it down is when I'm sleep-in' it off. ___

Pitches: B G D G

Chorus

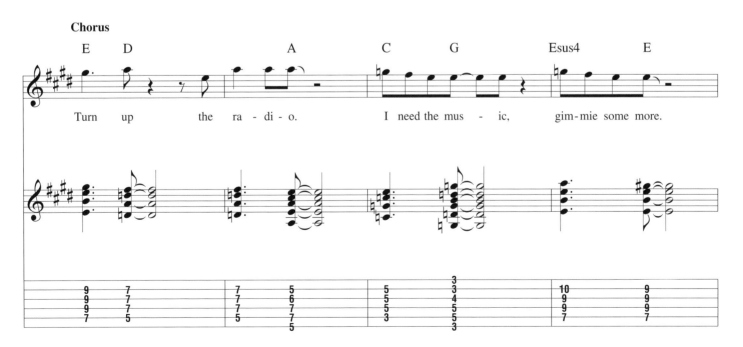

Turn up the ra - di - o. I need the mus - ic, gim-mie some more.

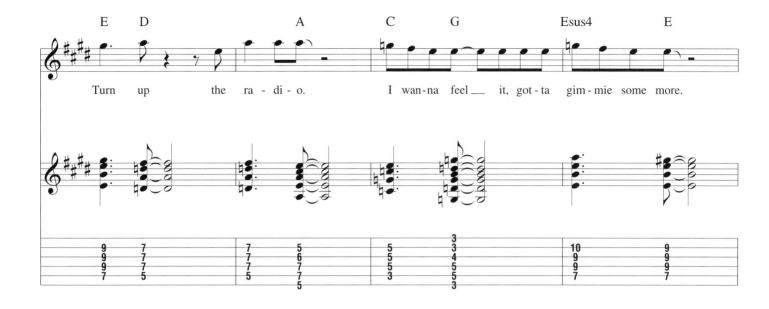

Turn up the ra - di - o. I wan-na feel __ it, got - ta gim-mie some more.

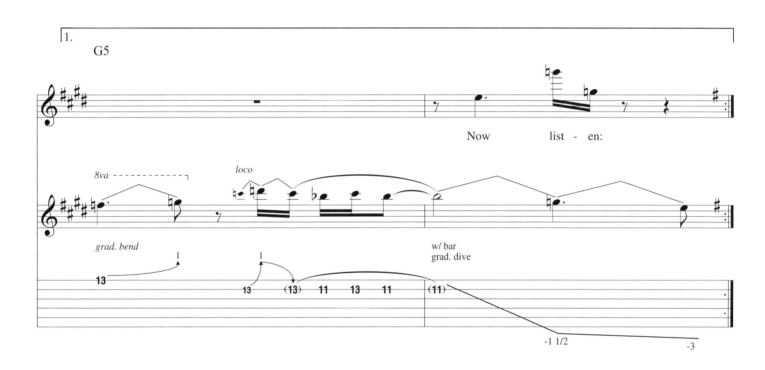

Now list - en:

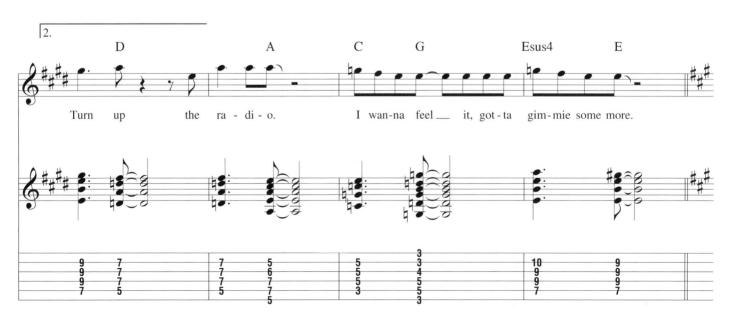

Turn up the ra - di - o. I wan-na feel __ it, got - ta gim-mie some more.

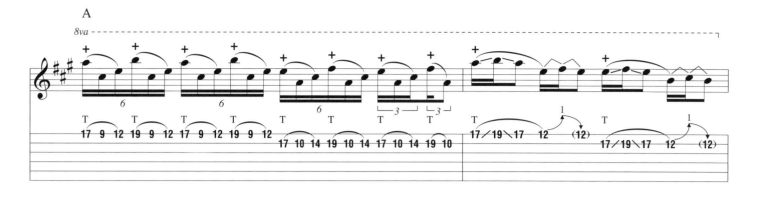

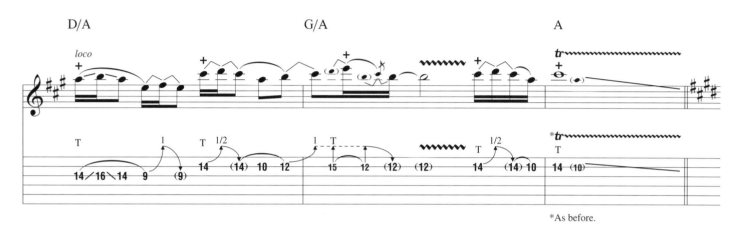

*As before.

Chorus

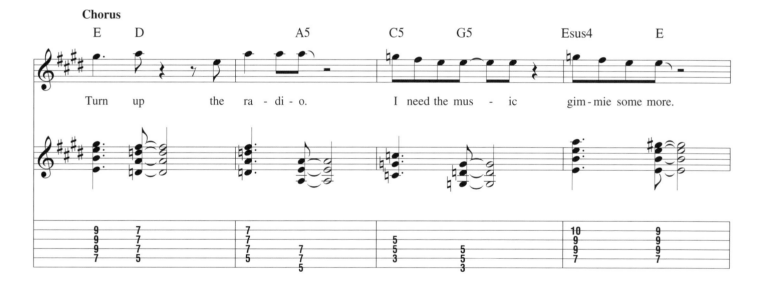

Turn up the ra - di - o. I need the mus - ic gim - mie some more.

Turn up the ra - di - o. I wan - na feel __ it, got - ta gim - mie some more.

Outro-Chorus

Turn up the ra - di - o. I need the mus - ic, gim - mie some more.

Repeat and fade

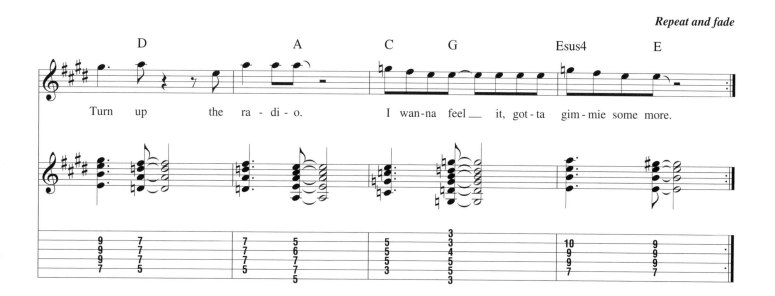

Turn up the ra - di - o. I wan - na feel __ it, got - ta gim - mie some more.

Additional Lyrics

2. I wanna shake, I wanna dance.
   So count it off, a, 1, 2, 3.
   I feel the beat, I'm in a trance;
   No better place to be.
   Daytime, nighttime, anytime.
   Things go better with Rock.
   I'm goin' 24 hours a day;
   I can't seem to stop.

We're Not Gonna Take It

Words and Music by Daniel Dee Snider

Intro
Moderate Rock ♩ = 149

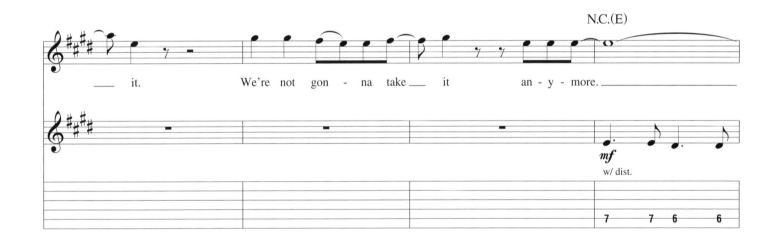

D.S. al Coda 1

Guitar Solo

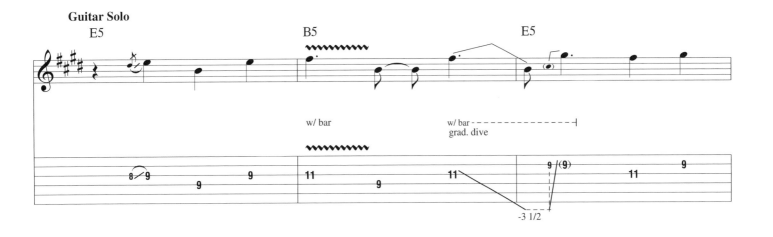

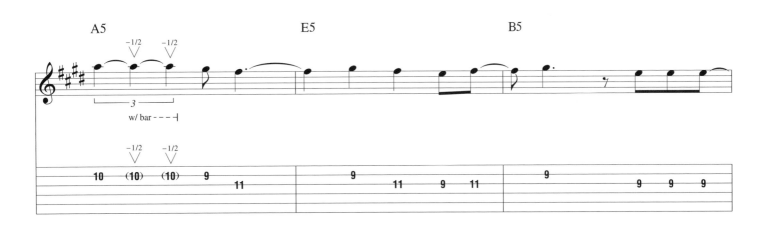

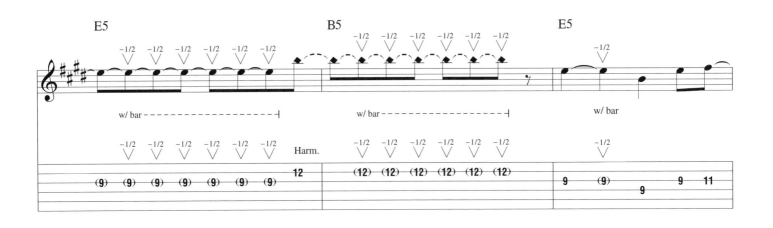

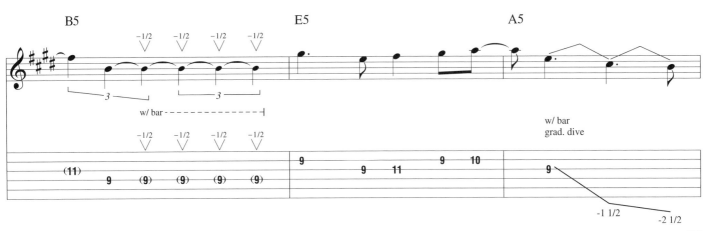

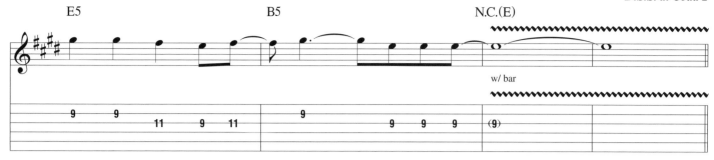

⊕ Coda 2

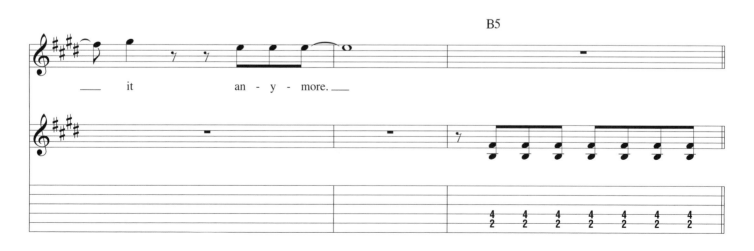

Chorus
w/ Voc. ad lib.

We're not gon - na take ___ it. No, we ain't gon - na take ___
___ it. We're not gon - na take ___ it an - y - more. ___

Repeat and fade

Additional Lyrics

2. Oh, you're so condescending.
Your gall is never-ending.
We don't want nothin'; not a thing from you.
Your life is trite and jaded,
Boring and confiscated.
If that's your best, your best won't do.

Nothin' but a Good Time

Words and Music by Bobby Dall, Brett Michaels, Bruce Johannesson and Rikki Rockett

Tune down 1/2 step:
(low to high) E♭-A♭-D♭-G♭-B♭-E♭

Intro
Moderate Rock ♩ = 132

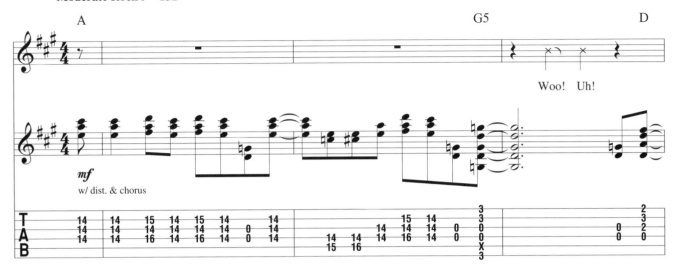

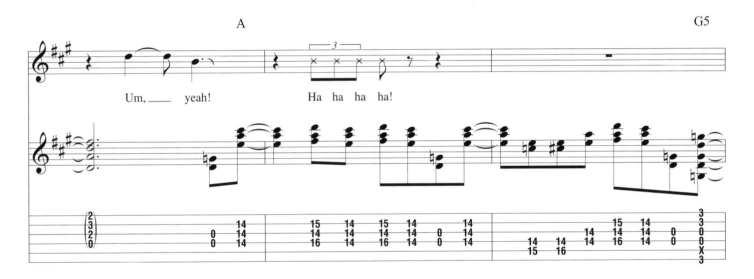

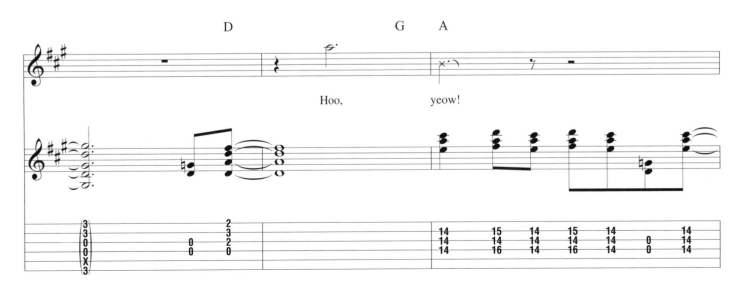

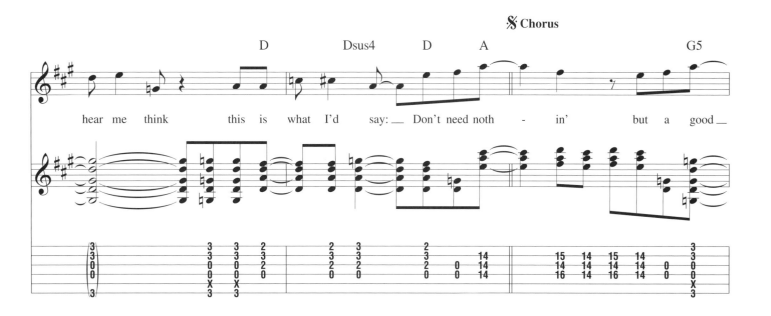

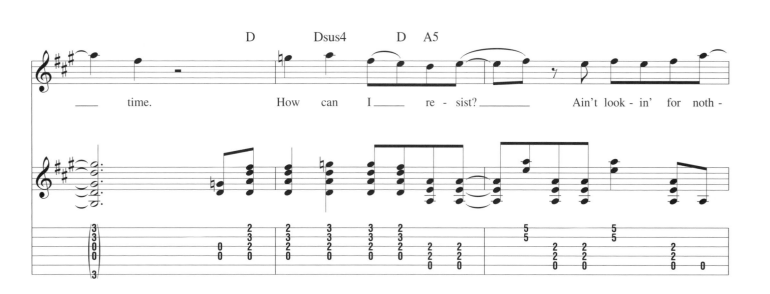

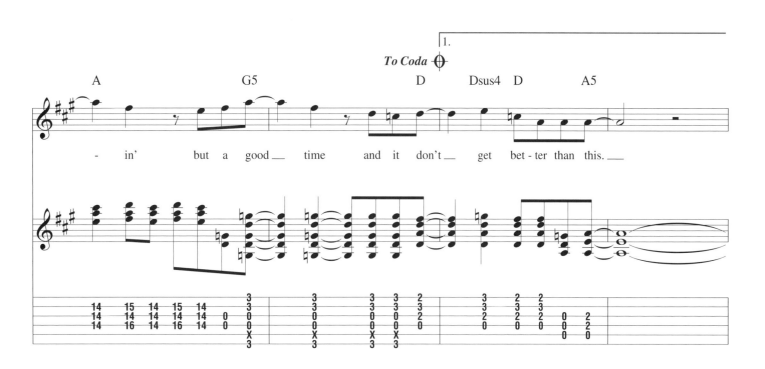

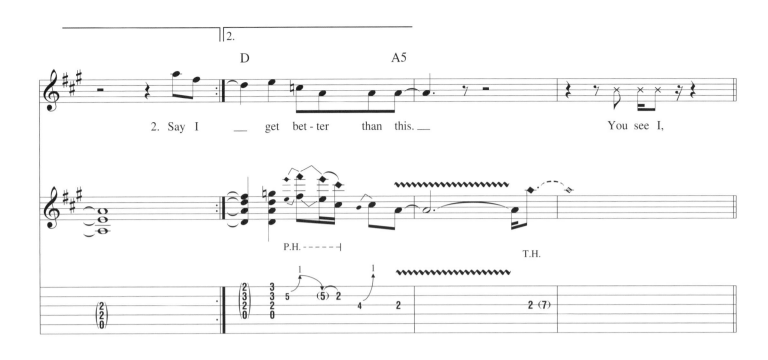

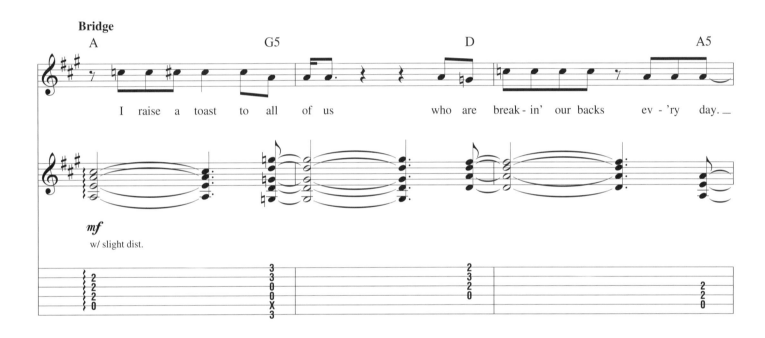

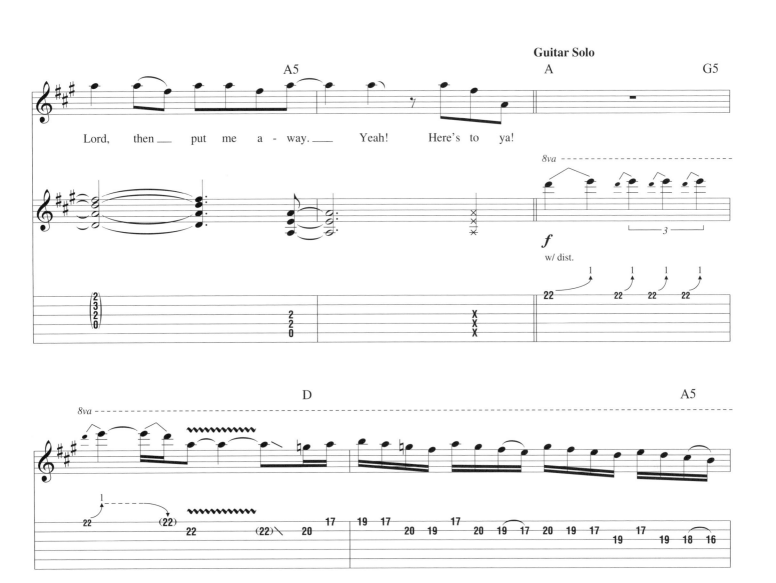

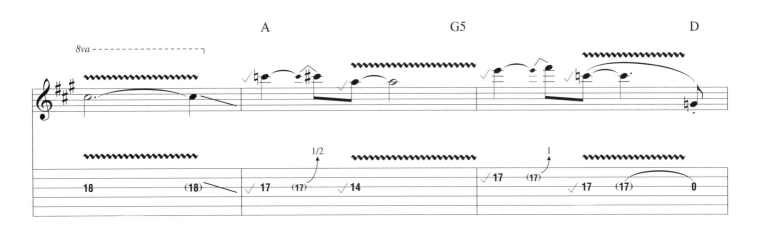

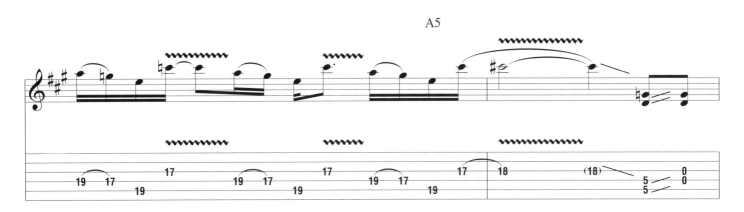

Lord, then put me a - way. Yeah! Here's to ya!

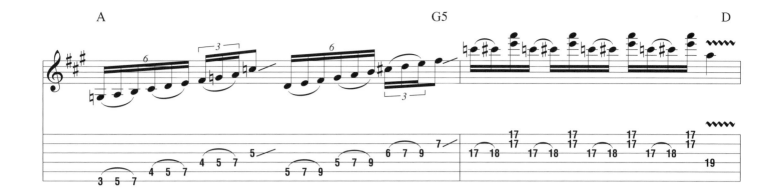

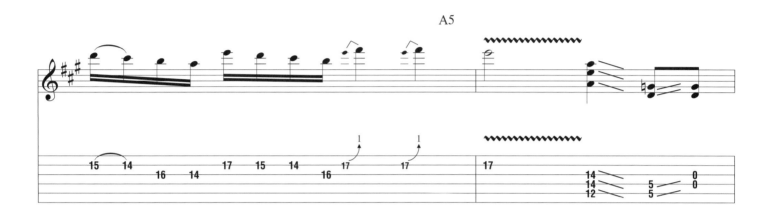

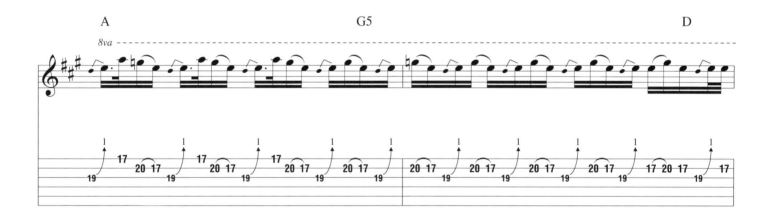

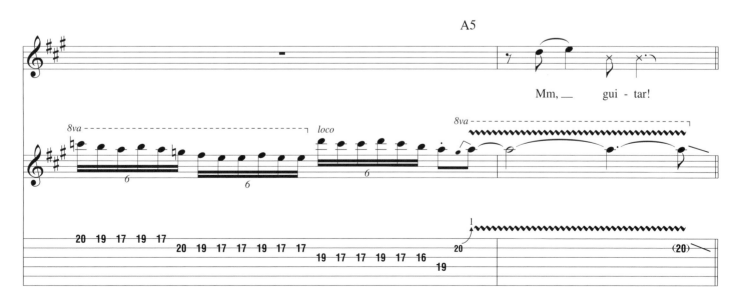

Mm, __ gui - tar!

Interlude

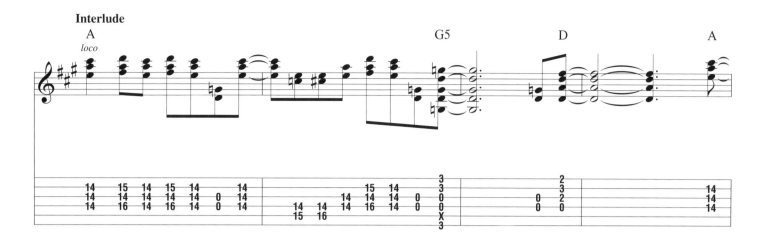

D.S. al Coda
(take 1st ending)

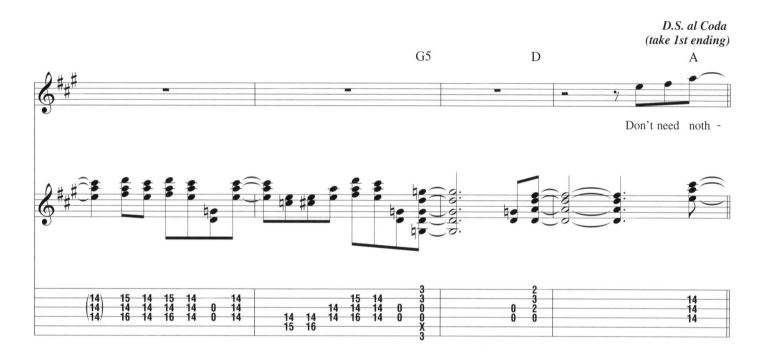

Don't need noth –

 Coda

Outro-Chorus

— get - ter than this. ___ Don't need noth – in' but a good ___

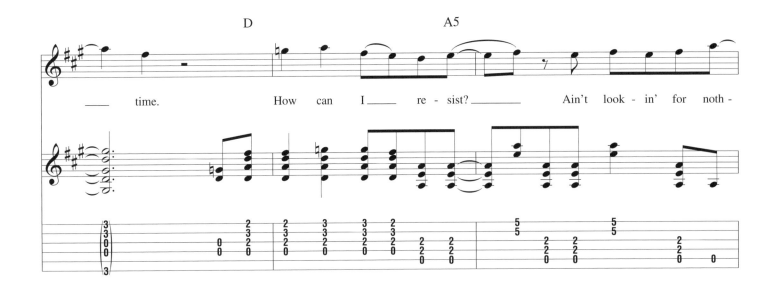

time. How can I ___ re - sist? ___ Ain't look - in' for noth -

- in' but a good ___ time and it don't ___ get bet - ter than this. ___

Free time

It don't get bet - ter, ba - by.

Additional Lyrics

2. Say I spend my money on women and wine,
But I couldn't tell you where I spent last night.
I'm real sorry 'bout the shape I'm in,
I just, uh, like my fun ev'ry now and then.

This series will help you play your favorite songs quickly and easily. Just follow the tab and listen to the CD to hear how the guitar should sound, and then play along using the separate backing tracks. Mac or PC users can also slow down the tempo without changing pitch by using the CD in their computer. The melody and lyrics are included in the book so that you can sing or simply follow along.

INCLUDES TAB

VOL. 1 – ROCK GUITAR 00699570 / $14.95
Day Tripper • Message in a Bottle • Refugee • Shattered • Sunshine of Your Love • Takin' Care of Business • Tush • Walk This Way.

VOL. 2 – ACOUSTIC 00699569 / $14.95
Angie • Behind Blue Eyes • Best of My Love • Blackbird • Dust in the Wind • Layla • Night Moves • Yesterday.

VOL. 3 – HARD ROCK 00699573 / $14.95
Crazy Train • Iron Man • Living After Midnight • Rock You like a Hurricane • Round and Round • Smoke on the Water • Sweet Child O' Mine • You Really Got Me.

VOL. 4 – POP/ROCK 00699571 / $14.95
Breakdown • Crazy Little Thing Called Love • Hit Me with Your Best Shot • I Want You to Want Me • Lights • R.O.C.K. in the U.S.A. • Summer of '69 • What I Like About You.

VOL. 5 – MODERN ROCK 00699574 / $14.95
Aerials • Alive • Bother • Chop Suey! • Control • Last Resort • Take a Look Around (Theme from M:I-2) • Wish You Were Here.

VOL. 6 – '90S ROCK 00699572 / $14.95
Are You Gonna Go My Way • Come Out and Play • I'll Stick Around • Know Your Enemy • Man in the Box • Outshined • Smells Like Teen Spirit • Under the Bridge.

VOL. 7 – BLUES GUITAR 00699575 / $14.95
All Your Love (I Miss Loving) • Born Under a Bad Sign • Hide Away • I'm Tore Down • I'm Your Hoochie Coochie Man • Pride and Joy • Sweet Home Chicago • The Thrill Is Gone.

VOL. 8 – ROCK 00699585 / $14.95
All Right Now • Black Magic Woman • Get Back • Hey Joe • Layla • Love Me Two Times • Won't Get Fooled Again • You Really Got Me.

VOL. 9 – PUNK ROCK 00699576 / $14.95
All the Small Things • Fat Lip • Flavor of the Weak • I Feel So • Lifestyles of the Rich and Famous• Say It Ain't So • Self Esteem • (So) Tired of Waiting for You.

VOL. 10 – ACOUSTIC 00699586 / $14.95
Here Comes the Sun • Landslide • The Magic Bus • Norwegian Wood (This Bird Has Flown) • Pink Houses • Space Oddity • Tangled Up in Blue • Tears in Heaven.

VOL. 11 – EARLY ROCK 00699579 / $14.95
Fun, Fun, Fun • Hound Dog • Louie, Louie • No Particular Place to Go • Oh, Pretty Woman • Rock Around the Clock • Under the Boardwalk • Wild Thing.

VOL. 12 – POP/ROCK 00699587 / $14.95
867-5309/Jenny • Every Breath You Take • Money for Nothing • Rebel, Rebel • Run to You • Ticket to Ride • Wonderful Tonight • You Give Love a Bad Name.

VOL. 13 – FOLK ROCK 00699581 / $14.95
Annie's Song • Leaving on a Jet Plane • Suite: Judy Blue Eyes • This Land Is Your Land • Time in a Bottle • Turn! Turn! Turn! • You've Got a Friend • You've Got to Hide Your Love Away.

VOL. 14 – BLUES ROCK 00699582 / $14.95
Blue on Black • Crossfire • Cross Road Blues (Crossroads) • The House Is Rockin' • La Grange • Move It on Over • Roadhouse Blues • Statesboro Blues.

VOL. 15 – R&B 00699583 / $14.95
Ain't Too Proud to Beg • Brick House • Get Ready • I Can't Help Myself • I Got You (I Feel Good) • I Heard It Through the Grapevine • My Girl • Shining Star.

VOL. 16 – JAZZ 00699584 / $14.95
All Blues • Bluesette • Footprints • How Insensitive • Misty • Satin Doll • Stella by Starlight • Tenor Madness.

VOL. 17 – COUNTRY 00699588 / $14.95
Amie • Boot Scootin' Boogie • Chattahoochee • Folsom Prison Blues • Friends in Low Places • Forever and Ever, Amen • T-R-O-U-B-L-E • Workin' Man Blues.

VOL. 18 – ACOUSTIC ROCK 00699577 / $14.95
About a Girl • Breaking the Girl • Drive • Iris • More Than Words • Patience • Silent Lucidity • 3 AM.

VOL. 19 – SOUL 00699578 / $14.95
Get Up (I Feel Like Being) a Sex Machine • Green Onions • In the Midnight Hour • Knock on Wood • Mustang Sally • Respect • (Sittin' On) the Dock of the Bay • Soul Man.

VOL. 20 – ROCKABILLY 00699580 / $14.95
Be-Bop-A-Lula • Blue Suede Shoes • Hello Mary Lou • Little Sister • Mystery Train • Rock This Town • Stray Cat Strut • That'll Be the Day.

VOL. 21 – YULETIDE 00699602 / $14.95
Angels We Have Heard on High • Away in a Manger • Deck the Hall • The First Noel • Go, Tell It on the Mountain • Jingle Bells • Joy to the World • O Little Town of Bethlehem.

VOL. 22 – CHRISTMAS 00699600 / $14.95
The Christmas Song • Frosty the Snow Man • Happy Xmas • Here Comes Santa Claus • Jingle-Bell Rock • Merry Christmas, Darling • Rudolph the Red-Nosed Reindeer • Silver Bells.

VOL. 23 – SURF 00699635 / $14.95
Let's Go Trippin' • Out of Limits • Penetration • Pipeline • Surf City • Surfin' U.S.A. • Walk Don't Run • The Wedge.

VOL. 24 – ERIC CLAPTON 00699649 / $14.95
Badge • Bell Bottom Blues • Change the World • Cocaine • Key to the Highway • Lay Down Sally • White Room • Wonderful Tonight.

VOL. 25 – LENNON & McCARTNEY 00699642 / $14.95
Back in the U.S.S.R. • Drive My Car • Get Back • A Hard Day's Night • I Feel Fine • Paperback Writer • Revolution • Ticket to Ride.

VOL. 26 – ELVIS PRESLEY 00699643 / $14.95
All Shook Up • Blue Suede Shoes • Don't Be Cruel • Heartbreak Hotel • Hound Dog • Jailhouse Rock • Little Sister • Mystery Train.

VOL. 27 – DAVID LEE ROTH 00699645 / $14.95
Ain't Talkin' 'Bout Love • Dance the Night Away • Hot for Teacher • Just Like Paradise • A Lil' Ain't Enough • Runnin' with the Devil • Unchained • Yankee Rose.

VOL. 28 – GREG KOCH 00699646 / $14.95
Chief's Blues • Death of a Bassman • Dylan the Villain • The Grip • Holy Grail • Spank It • Tonus Diabolicus • Zoiks.

VOL. 29 – BOB SEGER 00699647 / $14.95
Against the Wind • Betty Lou's Gettin' Out Tonight • Hollywood Nights • Mainstreet • Night Moves • Old Time Rock & Roll • Rock and Roll Never Forgets • Still the Same.

VOL. 30 – KISS 00699644 / $14.95
Cold Gin • Detroit Rock City • Deuce • Firehouse • Heaven's on Fire • Love Gun • Rock and Roll All Nite • Shock Me.

VOL. 31 – CHRISTMAS HITS 00699652 / $14.95
Blue Christmas • Do You Hear What I Hear • Happy Holiday • I Saw Mommy Kissing Santa Claus • I'll Be Home for Christmas • Let It Snow! Let It Snow! Let It Snow! • Little Saint Nick • Snowfall.

VOL. 32 – THE OFFSPRING 00699653 / $14.95
Bad Habit • Come Out and Play • Gone Away • Gotta Get Away • Hit That • The Kids Aren't Alright • Pretty Fly (For a White Guy) • Self Esteem.

VOL. 33 – ACOUSTIC CLASSICS 00699656 / $14.95
Across the Universe • Babe, I'm Gonna Leave You • Crazy on You • Heart of Gold • Hotel California • I'd Love to Change the World • Thick As a Brick • Wanted Dead or Alive.

VOL. 34 – CLASSIC ROCK 00699658 / $14.95
Aqualung • Born to Be Wild • The Boys Are Back in Town • Brown Eyed Girl • Reeling in the Years • Rock'n Me • Rocky Mountain Way • Sweet Emotion.

VOL. 35 – HAIR METAL 00699660 / $14.95
Decadence Dance • Don't Treat Me Bad • Down Boys • Seventeen • Shake Me • Up All Night • Wait • Talk Dirty to Me.

VOL. 36 – SOUTHERN ROCK 00699661 / $14.95
Can't You See • Flirtin' with Disaster • Hold on Loosely • Jessica • Mississippi Queen • Ramblin' Man • Sweet Home Alabama • What's Your Name.

VOL. 37 – ACOUSTIC METAL 00699662 / $14.95
Every Rose Has Its Thorn • Fly to the Angels • Hole Hearted • Love Is on the Way • Love of a Lifetime • Signs • To Be with You • When the Children Cry.

VOL. 38 – BLUES 00699663 / $14.95
Boom Boom • Cold Shot • Crosscut Saw • Everyday I Have the Blues • Frosty • Further On up the Road • Killing Floor • Texas Flood.

VOL. 39 – '80S METAL 00699664 / $14.95
Bark at the Moon • Big City Nights • Breaking the Chains • Cult of Personality • Lay It Down • Living on a Prayer • Panama • Smokin' in the Boys Room.

VOL. 40 – INCUBUS 00699668 / $14.95
Are You In? • Drive • Megalomaniac • Nice to Know You • Pardon Me • Stellar • Talk Shows on Mute • Wish You Were Here.

VOL. 41 – ERIC CLAPTON 00699669 / $14.95
After Midnight • Can't Find My Way Home • Forever Man • I Shot the Sheriff • I'm Tore Down • Pretending • Running on Faith • Tears in Heaven.

VOL. 42 – CHART HITS 00699670 / $14.95
Are You Gonna Be My Girl • Heaven • Here Without You • I Believe in a Thing Called Love • Just Like You • Last Train Home • This Love • Until the Day I Die.

VOL. 43 – LYNYRD SKYNYRD 00699681 / $14.95
Don't Ask Me No Questions • Free Bird • Gimme Three Steps • I Know a Little • Saturday Night Special • Sweet Home Alabama • That Smell • You Got That Right.

VOL. 44 – JAZZ 00699689 / $14.95
I Remember You • I'll Remember April • Impressions • In a Mellow Tone • Moonlight in Vermont • On a Slow Boat to China • Things Ain't What They Used to Be • Yesterdays.

VOL. 46 – MAINSTREAM ROCK 00699722 / $14.95
Just a Girl • Keep Away • Kryptonite • Lightning Crashes • 1979 • One Step Closer • Scar Tissue • Torn.

VOL. 47 – HENDRIX SMASH HITS 00699723/ $16.95
All Along the Watchtower • Can You See Me? • Crosstown Traffic • Fire • Foxey Lady • Hey Joe • Manic Depression • Purple Haze • Red House • Remember • Stone Free • The Wind Cries Mary.

VOL. 48 – AEROSMITH CLASSICS 00699724 / $14.95
Back in the Saddle • Draw the Line • Dream On • Last Child • Mama Kin • Same Old Song & Dance • Sweet Emotion • Walk This Way.

VOL. 50 – NÜ METAL 00699726 / $14.95
Duality • Here to Stay • In the End • Judith • Nookie • So Cold • Toxicity • Whatever.

VOL. 51 – ALTERNATIVE '90S 00699727 / $14.95
Alive • Cherub Rock • Come As You Are • Give It Away • Jane Says • No Excuses • No Rain • Santeria.

VOL. 56 – FOO FIGHTERS 00699749 / $14.95
All My Life • Best of You • DOA • I'll Stick Around • Learn to Fly • Monkey Wrench • My Hero • This Is a Call.

VOL. 57 – SYSTEM OF A DOWN 00699751 / $14.95
Aerials • B.Y.O.B. • Chop Suey! • Innervision • Question! • Spiders • Sugar • Toxicity.

Prices, contents, and availability subject to change without notice.

FOR MORE INFORMATION, SEE YOUR LOCAL MUSIC DEALER, OR WRITE TO:

HAL•LEONARD®
CORPORATION
7777 W. BLUEMOUND RD. P.O. BOX 13819 MILWAUKEE, WI 53213

Visit Hal Leonard online at www.halleonard.com

0106

RECORDED VERSIONS®
The Best Note-For-Note Transcriptions Available

ALL BOOKS INCLUDE TABLATURE

00692015 Aerosmith – Greatest Hits...........................$22.95	00692931 Jimi Hendrix – Axis: Bold As Love $22.95	00694975 Queen – Greatest Hits $24
00690603 Aerosmith – O Yeah! (Ultimate Hits) $24.95	00690608 Jimi Hendrix – Blue Wild Angel................$24.95	00690670 Queensryche – Very Best of......................$19
00690178 Alice in Chains – Acoustic $19.95	00692932 Jimi Hendrix – Electric Ladyland..............$24.95	00690878 The Raconteurs – Broken Boy Soldiers ...$19
00694865 Alice in Chains – Dirt $19.95	00690017 Jimi Hendrix – Live at Woodstock.............$24.95	00694910 Rage Against the Machine......................$19
00690387 Alice in Chains – Nothing Safe:	00690602 Jimi Hendrix – Smash Hits......................$19.95	00690055 Red Hot Chili Peppers –
The Best of the Box $19.95	00690843 H.I.M. – Dark Light $19.95	Blood Sugar Sex Magik $19
00690812 All American Rejects – Move Along............$19.95	00690869 Hinder – Extreme Behavior $19.95	00690584 Red Hot Chili Peppers – By the Way $19
00694932 Allman Brothers Band – Volume 1 ....$24.95	00690692 Billy Idol – Very Best of..........................$19.95	00690379 Red Hot Chili Peppers – Californication ...$19
00694933 Allman Brothers Band – Volume 2 ....$24.95	00690688 Incubus – A Crow Left of the Murder $19.95	00690673 Red Hot Chili Peppers – Greatest Hits $19
00694934 Allman Brothers Band – Volume 3 ....$24.95	00690457 Incubus – Make Yourself $19.95	00690852 Red Hot Chili Peppers –
00690865 Atreyu – A Deathgrip on Yesterday $19.95	00690544 Incubus – Morningview $19.95	Stadium Arcadium $24
00690609 Audioslave...$19.95	00690790 Iron Maiden Anthology $24.95	00690511 Django Reinhardt – Definitive Collection....$19
00690804 Audioslave – Out of Exile $19.95	00690730 Alan Jackson – Guitar Collection $19.95	00690779 Relient K – MMHMM............................$19
00690884 Audioslave – Revelations $19.95	00690721 Jet – Get Born $19.95	00690643 Relient K – Two Lefts Don't
00690820 Avenged Sevenfold – City of Evil $22.95	00690684 Jethro Tull – Aqualung $19.95	Make a Right...But Three Do $19
00690366 Bad Company – Original Anthology,	00690647 Jewel – Best of $19.95	00690631 Rolling Stones – Guitar Anthology...............$24
Book 1 ....$19.95	00690814 John5 – Songs for Sanity $19.95	00690685 David Lee Roth – Eat 'Em and Smile..........$19
00690503 Beach Boys – Very Best of..........................$19.95	00690751 John5 – Vertigo $19.95	00690694 David Lee Roth – Guitar Anthology............$24
00690489 Beatles – 1 ....$24.95	00690845 Eric Johnson – Bloom $19.95	00690031 Santana's Greatest Hits $19
00694929 Beatles – 1962-1966 ....$24.95	00690846 Jack Johnson and Friends – Sing-A-Longs and	00690796 Michael Schenker – Very Best of $19
00694930 Beatles – 1967-1970 ....$24.95	Lullabies for the Film Curious George $19.95	00690566 Scorpions – Best of $19
00694832 Beatles – For Acoustic Guitar $22.95	00690271 Robert Johnson – New Transcriptions........$24.95	00690604 Bob Seger – Guitar Collection $19
00690110 Beatles – White Album (Book 1) $19.95	00699131 Janis Joplin – Best of..............................$19.95	00690803 Kenny Wayne Shepherd Band – Best of $19
00692385 Chuck Berry...$19.95	00690427 Judas Priest – Best of..............................$19.95	00690857 Shinedown – Us and Them $19
00690835 Billy Talent –...$19.95	00690742 The Killers – Hot Fuss $19.95	00690530 Slipknot – Iowa....................................$19
00692200 Black Sabbath –	00694903 Kiss – Best of $24.95	00690733 Slipknot – Vol. 3 (The Subliminal Verses) ...$19
We Sold Our Soul for Rock 'N' Roll............$19.95	00690780 Korn – Greatest Hits, Volume 1 ....$22.95	00120004 Steely Dan – Best of................................$24
00690674 blink-182 ....$19.95	00690834 Lamb of God – Ashes of the Wake $19.95	00694921 Steppenwolf – Best of.............................$22
00690831 blink-182 – Greatest Hits $19.95	00690875 Lamb of God – Sacrament $19.95	00690655 Mike Stern – Best of.............................$19
00690491 David Bowie – Best of $19.95	00690823 Ray LaMontagne – Trouble $19.95	00690877 Stone Sour – Come What(ever) May $19
00690873 Breaking Benjamin – Phobia $19.95	00690679 John Lennon – Guitar Collection $19.95	00690520 Styx Guitar Collection $19
00690764 Breaking Benjamin – We Are Not Alone $19.95	00690781 Linkin Park – Hybrid Theory $22.95	00120081 Sublime...$19
00690451 Jeff Buckley – Collection $24.95	00690782 Linkin Park – Meteora $22.95	00690771 SUM 41 – Chuck $19
00690590 Eric Clapton – Anthology..........................$29.95	00690783 Live – Best of $19.95	00690767 Switchfoot – The Beautiful Letdown $19
00690415 Clapton Chronicles – Best of Eric Clapton ..$18.95	00690743 Los Lonely Boys $19.95	00690830 System of a Down – Hypnotize $19
00690074 Eric Clapton – The Cream of Clapton $24.95	00690876 Los Lonely Boys – Sacred $19.95	00690799 System of a Down – Mezmerize $19
00690716 Eric Clapton – Me and Mr. Johnson $19.95	00690720 Lostprophets – Start Something.................$19.95	00690531 System of a Down – Toxicity $19
00694869 Eric Clapton – Unplugged $22.95	00694954 Lynyrd Skynyrd – New Best of...................$19.95	00694824 James Taylor – Best of $16
00690162 The Clash – Best of $19.95	00690752 Lynyrd Skynyrd – Street Survivors.............$19.95	00690871 Three Days Grace – One-X $19
00690828 Coheed & Cambria – Good Apollo I'm Burning	00690577 Yngwie Malmsteen – Anthology................$24.95	00690737 3 Doors Down – The Better Life................$22
Star, IV, Vol. 1: From Fear Through the	00690754 Marilyn Manson – Lest We Forget $19.95	00690683 Robin Trower – Bridge of Sighs $19
Eyes of Madness $19.95	00694956 Bob Marley– Legend $19.95	00690740 Shania Twain – Guitar Collection................$19
00690593 Coldplay – A Rush of Blood to the Head.....$19.95	00694945 Bob Marley– Songs of Freedom $24.95	00699191 U2 – Best of: 1980-1990 ....$19
00690838 Cream – Royal Albert Hall:	00690657 Maroon5 – Songs About Jane $19.95	00690732 U2 – Best of: 1990-2000 ....$19
London May 2-3-5-6 2005 ....$22.95	00120080 Don McLean – Songbook $19.95	00690775 U2 – How to Dismantle an Atomic Bomb ...$22
00690856 Creed – Greatest Hits $22.95	00694951 Megadeth – Rust in Peace $22.95	00690575 Steve Vai – Alive in an Ultra World $22
00690401 Creed – Human Clay $19.95	00690768 Megadeth – The System Has Failed............$19.95	00660137 Steve Vai – Passion & Warfare $24
00690819 Creedence Clearwater Revival – Best of......$19.95	00690505 John Mellencamp – Guitar Collection.........$19.95	00690150 Stevie Ray Vaughan – Guitar Collection.......$24
00690572 Steve Cropper – Soul Man $19.95	00690646 Pat Metheny – One Quiet Night................$19.95	00660058 Stevie Ray Vaughan –
00690613 Crosby, Stills & Nash – Best of $19.95	00690558 Pat Metheny – Trio: 99>00 ....$19.95	Lightnin' Blues 1983-1987 ....$24
00690289 Deep Purple – Best of $17.95	00690040 Steve Miller Band – Young Hearts $19.95	00694835 Stevie Ray Vaughan – The Sky Is Crying ...$22
00690784 Def Leppard – Best of $19.95	00690794 Mudvayne – Lost and Found.....................$19.95	00690015 Stevie Ray Vaughan – Texas Flood $19
00690347 The Doors – Anthology $22.95	00690611 Nirvana $22.95	00690772 Velvet Revolver – Contraband....................$22
00690348 The Doors – Essential Guitar Collection $16.95	00694883 Nirvana – Nevermind $19.95	00690071 Weezer (The Blue Album) $19
00690810 Fall Out Boy – From Under the Cork Tree ..$19.95	00690026 Nirvana – Unplugged in New York............$19.95	00690447 The Who – Best of.................................$24
00690664 Fleetwood Mac – Best of $19.95	00690807 The Offspring – Greatest Hits $19.95	00690589 ZZ Top Guitar Anthology.......................$22
00690870 Flyleaf $19.95	00694847 Ozzy Osbourne – Best of $22.95	
00690808 Foo Fighters – In Your Honor $19.95	00690399 Ozzy Osbourne – Ozzman Cometh.............$19.95	
00690805 Robben Ford – Best of $19.95	00690866 Panic! At the Disco –	
00694920 Free – Best of $19.95	A Fever You Can't Sweat Out $19.95	
00690848 Godsmack – IV $19.95	00694855 Pearl Jam – Ten $19.95	
00690601 Good Charlotte –	00690439 A Perfect Circle – Mer De Noms...............$19.95	
The Young and the Hopeless $19.95	00690661 A Perfect Circle – Thirteenth Step.............$19.95	
00690697 Jim Hall – Best of $19.95	00690499 Tom Petty – Definitive Guitar Collection $19.95	
00690840 Ben Harper – Both Sides of the Gun $19.95	00690428 Pink Floyd – Dark Side of the Moon..........$19.95	
00694798 George Harrison – Anthology......................$19.95	00690789 Poison – Best of.....................................$19.95	
00692930 Jimi Hendrix – Are You Experienced?........$24.95	00693864 The Police – Best of................................$19.95